HUMAN RIGHTS

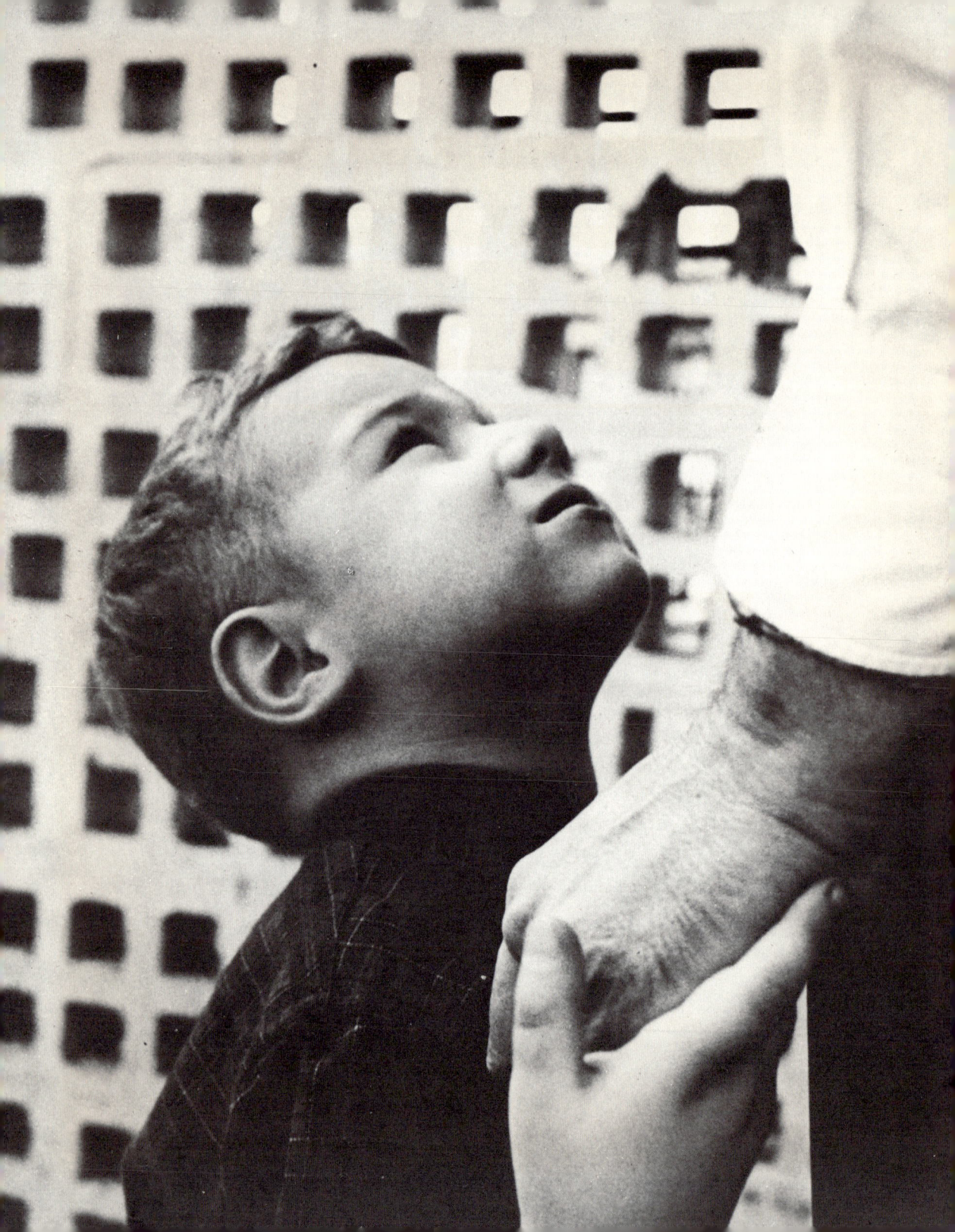

HUMAN RIGHTS

BY GERALD S. SNYDER

FRANKLIN WATTS
NEW YORK | LONDON | TORONTO | SYDNEY | 1980
A FIRST BOOK

Human rights are a major concern in the world today. Many organizations have provided material for this book. I would especially like to thank the United Nations Office of Public Information and International Year of the Child Secretariat, Freedom House, International Freedom to Publish Committee of the Association of American Publishers, P.E.N. American Center, the Human Rights Office of the National Council of Churches, and the International League for Human Rights.

GERALD S. SNYDER

Photographs courtesy of: UNICEF: frontispiece, pp. 11 (photo by Robison), 49, 50 (left), and 50 (right, photo by Robison); United Press International: pp. 18 (left), 24, 41, and 42; Wide World Photos: pp. 18 (right) and 29; United Nations: pp. 30 (photo by S. Rotner) and 57.

Map by Vantage Art, Inc.

Library of Congress Cataloging in Publication Data

Snyder, Gerald S
Human rights.

(A First book)
Includes index.
SUMMARY: Discusses the international status of civil rights and describes the struggles of women, racial minorities, children and the disabled to attain these rights in various countries. Also examines the role of the United Nations in securing human rights throughout the world.
1. Civil rights—Juvenile literature.
[1. Civil rights] I. Title.
JC571.S687   323.4   79-26031
ISBN 0-531-04103-4

Copyright © 1980 by Gerald S. Snyder
All rights reserved
Printed in the United States of America
5 4 3 2

CONTENTS

WHAT ARE HUMAN RIGHTS?
1

POLITICAL RIGHTS
8

FREEDOM OF EXPRESSION
14

RACIAL DISCRIMINATION
20

RELIGIOUS FREEDOM
32

WOMEN'S RIGHTS
37

CHILDREN'S RIGHTS
AND RIGHTS OF
THE HANDICAPPED
46

WHAT CAN THE
UNITED NATIONS DO?
55

INDEX
61

HUMAN RIGHTS

WHAT ARE HUMAN RIGHTS?

Ahmed Mobuto is a black man. He lives in Africa in a country where most of the people are black. He has a wife and two children—a girl, age twelve, and a boy, ten—who attend school with other black youths.

One day Ahmed decided to keep his children home from school in protest against the school system. He did not like the fact that the government did not allow his daughter and son to sit together with white children and receive an equal education.

Ahmed went to a rally with other black parents who felt just as he did. "Equal rights, human rights—they must be the goal of all people," he heard someone say. But soon the sound of dogs growling drowned out the voice of the speaker. Gunshots pierced the air. Uniformed police appeared out of nowhere and Ahmed felt himself being pushed with others into a van. There was a hurried ride to a prison, where Ahmed heard that he would be tried as a "terrorist." The country's security was being threatened by people like him, he was told.

Ahmed is not real. The events just related did not actually occur. But they could have, for in many parts of the world today people are being persecuted for openly professing their beliefs. Many people cannot observe their religion without fear of being arrested. Many people cannot vote. Many people cannot leave their country when they wish. Many governments control the news that comes out of their country. Writers have been shot. Publishers have been threatened. Property has been confiscated, jobs denied, innocent people killed.

According to Freedom House, an American organization dedicated to bringing greater freedom to oppressed—not free—peoples, in only 35 percent of all the 155 nations and 58 related territories in the world are the citizens free to choose their leaders and their government. In only that small percentage can people go to a courtroom for help and receive news and information that is not controlled—censored—by the government. Almost 40 percent of the world's population is "not free," and 25 percent is only "partly free," says Freedom House. A Map of Freedom, published in 1979 by Freedom House, shows free countries in white, partly free ones shaded, and those that are considered not free in black. As you can see, huge areas of the world appear in black. In many parts of Asia, Africa, and South America, there are only scattered shaded and white spots—the picture is almost entirely black.

Of the fifty nations of Africa, only four are classified as free—Djibouti, Gambia, Botswana, and Mauritius—and no fewer than thirty are judged not free. The other sixteen nations are partly free.

An indication of a basic lack of human rights almost always can be found in countries where men, women, and children are fleeing, fleeing their own countries. In their native lands, for example, these people may not have the right to vote. So, it might be said, they vote with their feet—they leave.

The most-free countries of the world, says Freedom House, are (in alphabetical order) Australia, Austria, the Bahamas, Barbados, Belgium, Canada, Costa Rica, Denmark, France, West Germany, Iceland, Ireland, Luxembourg, the Netherlands, New Zealand, Norway, Sweden, Switzerland, the United Kingdom, the United States, and Venezuela.

This is not to say that in other countries people do not enjoy any basic human rights, such as the right to vote or the right to speak out on public issues. But it is clear that in many of these countries, some human rights are in peril.

Human rights are rights so basic that people cannot live like human beings without them. The rights to feed and shelter ourselves are human rights. But the idea of human rights reaches far beyond biological needs. For at the heart of the meaning of human rights lies the *dignity* of each human being.

According to the United Nations, which in 1948 adopted the Universal Declaration of Human Rights, human rights are "those conditions of life which allow us fully to develop and use our human qualities of intelligence and conscience and to satisfy our spiritual needs. Human rights are fundamental to our nature; without them, we cannot live as human beings."

Over the last thirty years, particularly in the United States, much has been said and written about *civil* rights—the right,

THE MAP OF FREEDOM

January 1978

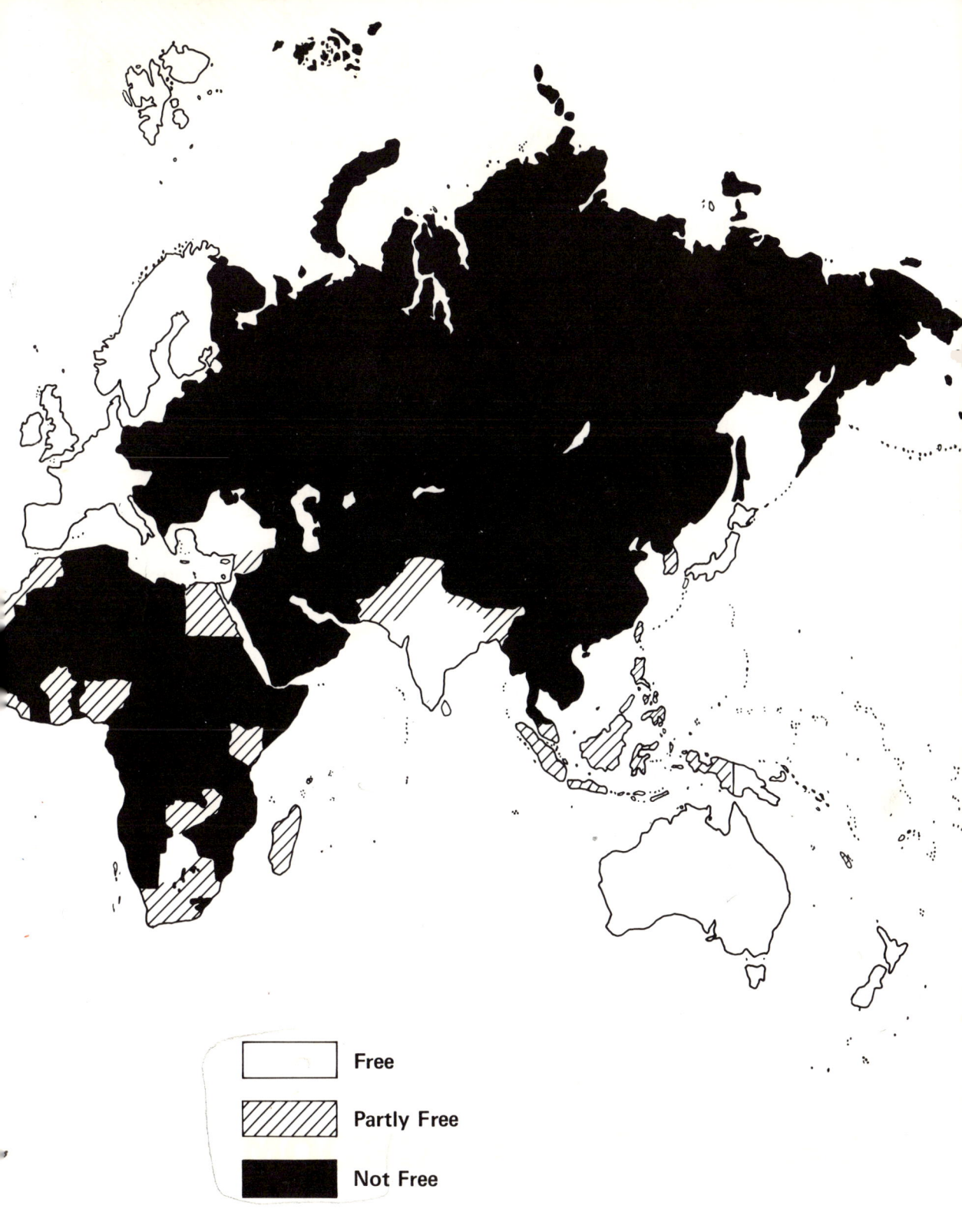

for instance, of black children to enjoy the same educational opportunities as white children, and the right of all black (and white) citizens to equal housing and employment opportunities.

Civil rights *are* human rights. But they are only one kind. The right to live without fear of imprisonment for holding unpopular beliefs, the right to enter and leave one's country at will, and the right to worship as one wishes are also human rights.

From the beginning of civilized life, human beings have fought for human rights. At the core of the struggle has been the belief that people—and governments—should do only that which is *moral*, a word which, according to the dictionary, means "of or relating to principles of right and wrong," or "virtuous, righteous, and noble." Thus, *morality* means conforming to the rules of right conduct, and right conduct is the heart of human rights.

For years the United States has denied economic and military aid to countries that seriously violated the human rights of their citizens. But not until 1977 did human rights become a subject of widespread discussion and debate in America. In that year, under the leadership of President Jimmy Carter, the government gave up its policy of "quiet diplomacy" with other nations and began to speak out openly, drawing world attention to the problem.

"Because we are free," Carter said in his inaugural address, "we can never be indifferent to the fate of freedom elsewhere. Our moral sense dictates a clear-cut preference for those societies which share with us an abiding respect for individual human rights."

The most basic of these rights, Carter said, is the right to be free from violence, violence inflicted by governments, terrorists, criminals, "or self-appointed messiahs operating under the cover of politics or religion."

Later, in a White House speech given before hundreds of human rights workers and members of Congress, Carter said, "Our pursuit of human rights is part of a broad effort to use our great power and influence in the service of creating a better world—a world in which human beings can live in peace, in freedom, and with their basic needs adequately met. Human rights is the soul of our foreign policy—because human rights is the very soul of our sense of nationhood."

Under President Carter the United States began to pursue this pledge in earnest. Countries that mistreated their citizens were publicly criticized. Many nations were angered by this policy. America should not tell other countries how to govern themselves, some people said. But human rights groups were pleased. For suddenly, people everywhere were talking about human rights. As one human rights leader put it: "For years we were preachers, cockeyed idealists, or busybodies—but now we are respectable."

POLITICAL RIGHTS

In our view of an ideal or perfect world, all people would live without fear of imprisonment for political beliefs and without any restrictions on their right to vote or to speak out on government activities.

However, there are very few perfect societies in this far too imperfect world. In fact, in some countries, not only is dissent—public disagreement with government policy—discouraged, but dissenters are tortured for their practices. The soles of a victim's feet may be beaten. A suspect may be forced to sit naked for hours on a metal bar. Electric charges may be applied to the ears or the mouth or another sensitive part of the body. In one country, a playwright charged that nails were driven through his feet—and showed his wounds to prove it. His crime? Writing plays the government did not like.

Political rights are those rights that relate to the affairs of government. A person may express these rights by voting for leaders or by speaking out on political issues. In most Communist countries—the Soviet Union, Communist China, and Cuba, for example—there is a dictator, and ordinary citizens have no voting power. In democracies such as the United States, the power to choose leaders is held by the citizenry, who express their wishes through regularly held elections.

Communist countries are generally very harsh with political dissenters. Some even follow dissenters who have fled, in order to quiet them. In Britain, detectives from Scotland Yard investigated the mysterious deaths of two Communist refugees. Found in the bodies of both men were tiny pellets, believed to have come from the poisoned darts of foreign agents.

In some countries there are "death squads," police units whose job it is to kill dissenters. Elsewhere, accused criminals have been beaten to death without that most basic of human rights—the right to a fair trial. The enemies of some governments have been shot down on the street. Students handing out antigovernment leaflets have been put to death for their "crime."

In the African country of Uganda, where a cruel dictator ruled for more than eight years, it is estimated that some 300,000 people were executed or just murdered outright. Many had their skulls crushed with steel hammers.

Why this reign of terror, this obvious thirst for blood? Because the Ugandan dictator, Idi Amin, suspected the victims of opposing his regime. Only when Amin was overthrown, in mid-1979, did the massacres in Uganda stop.

To us, the violation of human rights is obviously wrong. Why, then, you may wonder, do we allow it to go on?

One reason is that different countries, or different governments, have different notions of just what an ideal society is. Although most governments profess a respect for human rights—and have even signed international treaties guaranteeing to respect human rights—many of these governments apply their own definition to the concept of human rights. And all of these governments have *sovereignty*—the right to govern their own territory. It is precisely for these reasons that the subject of human rights is so sensitive.

Many poor nations claim human rights for their people. But human rights to them are not always the same as they are to wealthier nations such as the United States and Great Britain. Most of us think of human rights in terms of freedom of speech or perhaps freedom of the press. Many poorer countries, especially those in Asia, Africa, and Latin America, tend to view human rights as only those rights that affect jobs, housing, food, and education. "In much of the world," as one American official stated the problem, "the chief human right that people recognize is eight hundred calories a day."

However, even in some prosperous nations there is a resistance to the ideals of liberty as viewed by the West.

Take the case of the Soviet Union. For years the Soviet police have been arresting Russian intellectuals who openly disagree with the policies of the government. Some of these

This little Nigerian boy, surrounded by adults, doesn't stand a very good chance of getting his share of this United Nations food handout. In poorer nations, winning human rights often means mostly just getting enough to eat.

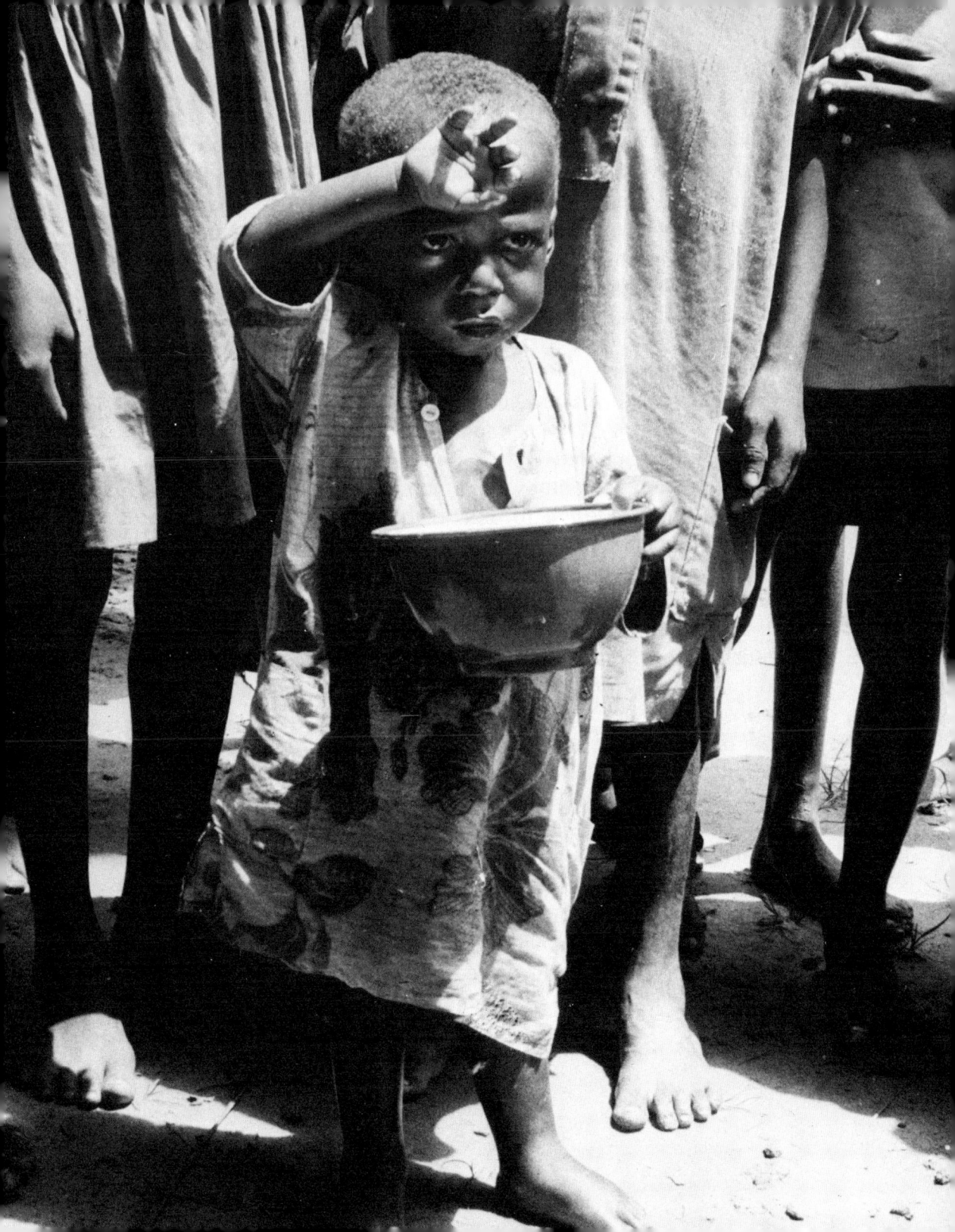

intellectuals have been charged with terrorism. Others have been put in hospitals for treatment of "mental illness." Yet the government insists that Soviet citizens do indeed have the right to criticize their government. The question in the Russian view is, how do they criticize? Do they do it in a "conscientious" manner or do they do it in a "deluded" manner, merely to stir up trouble and be offensive and insulting to the government?

In completely free societies, these distinctions are not made. Opposition is allowed, freedom of speech is permitted, and government by the people—democracy—is encouraged.

It should be noted here that even some countries inclined toward democracy have at times felt free to suspend human rights, in order to defend themselves against real or imagined revolutionaries.

Should all countries interpret human rights the same way?

At a news conference in the White House in 1978, President Carter said: "We have a deep commitment in our nation to the enhancement of human rights, not only here but around the world." It is clear that Carter was referring to the *American* interpretation of human rights and would like to see the United States take a more active role in this area.

But others are not so sure. James William Fulbright, the former chairman of the U.S. Senate Foreign Relations Committee, had this to say: "Americans like to think of themselves as a very superior, unique people. We hope other countries will move toward values that we approve. But the Chinese have entirely different values—have had them for two thousand years—concerning the relationship of the individual to the state. Should we ask them to change?"

Senator Fulbright was not condoning the terrorism that takes place in some countries—that is, the killing or harassment of innocent people who happen to have ideas that are different from those of the government in power. But his statement does show us another viewpoint—and helps us to see why free nations should not be too quick to impose their definition of human rights on other governments.

In 1821 John Quincy Adams was the U.S. Secretary of State. Adams supported freedom and independence, but he warned Americans against the dangers of trying to force American standards and ideals on other countries. America should support freedom and independence everywhere with "her heart, her benedictions, and her prayers," he said, but should not "go abroad in search of monsters to destroy."

FREEDOM OF EXPRESSION

Ulla Allgier, journalist; arrested and imprisoned, present status unknown. Oscar Barros, writer; whereabouts unknown. Mainul Hossain, editor; arrested and imprisoned, present status unknown. Renato Tapajos, filmmaker; imprisoned. Paulo Wright, teacher; detained without charges. Carmen Bueno, actress and scriptwriter; abducted and imprisoned, believed tortured. Gonzalo Toro Garland, poet and composer; imprisoned.

These are the names of real people, and the list—supplied by International P.E.N., an association of poets, playwrights, essayists, editors, and novelists, with offices in Europe, Asia, Africa, Australia, and North and South America—goes on and on. Repression refers to the enforced prevention of a person from expressing his or her ideas. The "Freedom to Write" global report, which was issued in 1978 and which contains the names listed above, actually cites a total of 606 individual cases of repression in 55 separate countries.

Not only are writers on the list but also included are translators and television and radio commentators, as well as relatives of these people. The list includes 471 persons who were imprisoned and 22 who were confined to psychiatric institutions or placed under house arrest—forced to remain in their homes. The whereabouts of 61 other persons are reported as unknown.

Individuals listed as imprisoned without an exact sentence "have usually been detained without charges or trial," says P.E.N. "It should also be noted that sometimes when an individual has been abducted or has disappeared, it is later discovered that the victim has been imprisoned."

Not on the list, says P.E.N., are writers who have been murdered or tortured to death or blacklisted—prevented from publishing their work or finding employment. Also not mentioned are those whose homes have been bombed or whose families have been harassed or threatened with violence.

The victims are dissimilar, but they all have one thing in common: the desire to possess the fundamental human right known as freedom of expression. In many cases this means, as might be expected, the freedom to write or to distribute literature about the oppressive policies of their governments. But this is not always the case.

For example, Eugenio Suarez, an editor from Spain, was reportedly arrested for "showing disrespect for the military." Thomas Steinberger, a writer from the German Democratic Republic (East Germany), was arrested and imprisoned for trying to "escape" from his country. Others, mostly writers and editors, have been arrested and charged with sexual misconduct.

"Imprisoned." "Abducted." "Arrested." "Tortured." "Disappeared." "Detained." "Banned." The words explode like bombs through the P.E.N. report. Even in the United States there have been some cases of repression concerning writers, contends P.E.N. The association cites a number of American editors, publishers, and bookstore owners who have been sentenced to prison terms for dealing in material the courts have judged to be obscene—that is, material designed to incite lust or depravity.

Human rights are violated to some extent under all government systems. But most observers agree that nowhere else in the world is there more freedom of expression than in the United States. This is because the Constitution, that basic charter of the American government, guarantees to all citizens the freedom to speak and write as they please. According to the Constitution's First Amendment, Congress shall make no law abridging—lessening—freedom of speech or of the press.

In only about 30 percent of the nations of the world is there a truly free press. But why should there be, anywhere in the world, the fear of words, written or spoken?

Because words are the describers of life. Writers use them as the means for telling the truth as they see it.

In many countries run by dictators the government controls the press. Information is regarded as a tool of the state. Reporters must rely on the government for news handouts. They are denied free access to the sources of their choice. They are restricted in their travel. They are subjected to punishment if the government does not like what they write.

In some countries books and pamphlets that contain antigovernment sentiments are burned.

In the Soviet Union, books about prison conditions and violations of human rights are banned. Nowhere in Russia will there be found, for example, any public display of Aleksandr Solzhenitsyn's Nobel prize-winning book *The Gulag Archipelago,* an account of prison camp conditions during the rule of dictator Joseph Stalin.

It also is held a crime in the Soviet Union to circulate antigovernment literature received from abroad. In mid-1978, for example, Alexander Ginzburg, a founding member of a Russian human rights group, was sentenced to eight years in prison for having distributed such materials. (However, by an agreement with the United States, Ginzburg and four other Russian dissidents were released from prison in April 1979. In exchange for the five, the United States freed two Russian spies.)

In another recent case, the Association of American Publishers (AAP) and the International Publishers Association publicly protested the trial of Russian physicist and fighter for human rights Yuri Orlov, accused of writing and passing out anti-Soviet materials. Orlov spent fifteen months in prison before he was finally brought to trial.

Speaking of the AAP's efforts to help writers, its president, Winthrop Knowlton, said: "When you have come to know and perhaps even love an author who has been in prison or who is living in desperate circumstances with his family—sometimes ill, unable to purchase medicines—all because of his ideas and his books and you have published his books—well, the experience changes you and you begin to wonder whether you really can ever do enough to help."

A writer named Bertolt Brecht once wrote a poem on the

Left: Aleksandr Solzhenitsyn, Nobel prize-winning Russian author and dissident. Right: Yuri Orlov, Russian physicist and dissident.

importance of free expression that told of a poet whose work had been left off a list of those to be burned. Brecht's poem said, in part:

He rushed to his writing table
On wings of anger and wrote a letter to those in power.
Burn me, he wrote with hurrying pen, burn me!
Do not treat me in this fashion. Don't leave me out.
Have I not
Always spoken the truth in my books? And now
You treat me like a liar! I order you:
Burn me!

Books *can* be burned. But ideas cannot. As long as there is truth that needs to be revealed, a way will be found to reveal it.

RACIAL DISCRIMINATION

Apartheid means separateness. It is a word in Afrikaans, one of the official languages of South Africa. But in that nation apartheid does not refer to just any kind of separateness. It is used to describe the government's policy of racial segregation, perhaps the most heated human rights issue in the world.

In South Africa certain areas have been designated as "colored" and others as "white." "Pass laws" require every African man or woman over the age of sixteen to carry a "reference book" showing that he or she has permission to work or to seek work and naming the type of work for which the holder is entitled to apply. The pass laws have succeeded in preventing more than half the country's 18.6 million blacks (compared to 4.4 million whites) from leaving their more undeveloped tribal regions.

Any establishment of "mixed" worker unions consisting of both white and black employees is not allowed. South African blacks can easily find work in the gold and diamond mines, but a system of "job reservation" based on race bars them from employment in certain professions. Whites hold the best jobs, earn more money, and are given the best opportunities for advancement.

In South Africa newspapers are almost entirely white-owned. There are "white" theatres and "colored" theatres, "white" taxis and "colored" taxis. "White only" and "Colored only" signs abound. A black visitor to South Africa might be permitted to use a "white only" vehicle, but only as an "honorary white," a term used often in that country. In some instances the term "colored" is being replaced with the term "black" or "Afrikaan." But the effect remains the same.

South Africa is not the only nation to promote racial discrimination. The doctrine of white supremacy, for instance, has also been associated with the African nation of Zimbabwe-Rhodesia. There the whites, who make up only a little more than 4 percent of the population, have for years dominated the black majority. Only recently have blacks risen to power in the government. And only recently has official segregation in housing, education, health services, and public places ended. There, thanks to new laws, white government schools are at last beginning to be integrated. Blacks can now enter white hospitals and move into white suburbs. They can own or rent property that previously only whites could own or rent.

Yet in Zimbabwe-Rhodesia, when the news was announced, there was no dancing in the streets. Blacks took the news calmly. For they knew that the granting of human rights does not necessarily mean that these rights will be enjoyed. The racial barriers were down—but only for those who could afford it. Most of Zimbabwe-Rhodesia's blacks do not have the money to take advantage of their new rights. They can attend the white schools—if they can afford to own or rent property in the white school districts. An average black person would have to pay all the money he or she earned in an entire month to rent a modest home in a white community. Blacks can be admitted to white hospitals—if they can afford the high cost of treatment, drugs, and beds. And so on.

Thus, even when racial barriers fall, there may be economic barriers to human rights.

Still, the situation in Zimbabwe-Rhodesia is an advance over the situation in South Africa.

Countries throughout the world have denounced apartheid. Many people have spoken and demonstrated against it. Petitions have been signed. Books have been written. And international pressure of many other kinds has been brought to bear on South Africa.

One of the most effective strategies has come through the world of sports. When foreign athletes began to snub South African athletes, refusing to participate with them in international tennis and football competitions, South Africa was forced to moderate some of its policies on racial segregation.

Many white South Africans do not understand the scorn they have aroused. "Why blame us?" they ask. "There is plenty of prejudice in the world. Why pick on us?"

To understand why South Africans are so puzzled by the criticism heaped upon them, it is important to understand how deeply rooted the feeling of white supremacy is in South Africa. As one South African-born writer explained: "Apartheid does not give in easily to political pressure because it is not a conventional political system—it is so different. It is a religious faith, deeply held and deeply kept; it was born the day the first white man set foot in South Africa."

Another reason why apartheid continues to exist is that it provides the economy with large numbers of people who will work for low pay. About half of the work force in the "white" areas of the country are black migrants—people forced to leave their families and keep moving in order to find work. In the view of many observers, this is just the government's intention—in order to prevent the blacks from becoming a stable political force.

Does apartheid exist in countries outside Africa? In a sense, yes, even in countries with constitutions that guarantee the equality of all citizens. For whenever a person is denied employment or other opportunities because of the shade of his or her skin, a *type* of apartheid might be said to be in existence.

In the United States, for example, black people have had to undergo a long struggle to achieve dignity and justice. The abolition of slavery in 1863 did little to provide American blacks with equal rights or equal opportunities. Nearly ninety years passed without any significant gains in these areas. Then came World War II, and the blacks, who had fought valiantly side by side with whites to protect democracy and their country, were no longer willing to resume an unequal position at home. In the 1950s and 1960s, led by men such as the Reverend Martin Luther King, Jr., and the Reverend Ralph Abernathy, they began demanding their rights and were determined to be heard. They staged sit-ins, demonstrations, boycotts—anything that would focus national attention on themselves and on their lack of civil—human—rights. They were

Martin Luther King, Jr., addressing a civil rights rally in Chicago in 1964.

arrested, harassed, and threatened, but the black "revolution" was on.

The government reacted. In 1960, the U.S. Department of Justice sued three states—Georgia, Alabama, and Louisiana—for failing to register qualified black voters. That same year Congress passed a civil rights bill requiring that voting records be kept so that they could be checked for any wrongdoing. Two years later, Congress also ordered an end to discrimination in federally funded housing. And for the first time, blacks were appointed to some important federal positions.

Discrimination did not end, however, and new pressures had to be exerted. The Student Nonviolent Coordinating Committee and the Southern Christian Leadership Conference joined the battle for greater civil and human rights for blacks. The National Association for the Advancement of Colored People (NAACP) became strong and influential at this time. The Interracial Congress of Racial Equality (CORE) began sending "freedom riders" into the South to test new desegregation laws. Riots erupted on college campuses to protest the fact that blacks were still being excluded from white colleges and universities. Many people were killed or injured.

In 1963, in a national radio and television address, President John F. Kennedy said, "We face a moral crisis as a country and as a people. It cannot be met by repressive police action. It cannot be left to increased demonstrations in the streets. It cannot be quieted by token moves or talk. It is a time to act in the Congress, in your state and local legislative body and, above all, in all of our daily lives."

Congress did act, passing the Civil Rights Act of 1964. This act was the most far-reaching law in American history in support of racial equality. Among other measures, it banned discrimination in public places, established a federal Equal Employment Opportunity Commission, and gave financial aid to communities that were desegregating their schools.

It seemed as if things were really changing for American blacks and that the black movement would continue to grow in strength until it had swept away all traces of discrimination. Then, in 1968, Martin Luther King, Jr., was assassinated. King had worked hard to bring all groups within the black movement together to work for the common good. After his death, the various factions seemed to split apart. Many continued to fight for equality, some using violent means, others choosing to work through the courts or their government legislatures. But the unity that had accomplished so much was gone.

In the 1970s, some changes were brought about, but not nearly enough to solve a new problem that was rapidly developing and making the achievement of equality even more difficult for blacks. This new problem? Blacks moving to the cities in great numbers to find work, where little work was available. And as blacks moved in, whites moved out, causing the economy to falter and black ghettos to form—overcrowded, unsafe, and poor.

Today, more than fifteen years after the Civil Rights Act was passed, segregation is still prevalent in America. Blacks continue to move into the cities, and whites continue to move out. In America's capital, Washington, D.C., more than 96 percent of all public school pupils are blacks or members of another minority. In Atlanta, Georgia, minorities form 89 percent of the student population, in Detroit, Michigan, 82 percent, and so on. Busing—the moving of students from one school to another farther away to achieve a racial mix—is at best only partially effective. And it is often met with a great deal of resistance.

So the dream of true integration, of blacks and whites living together in peace and their children sitting down to learn together, is still mostly just a dream.

To help blacks and other minority group members achieve equality in the area of job opportunity, the government in recent years has encouraged—and sometimes even ordered—many of the country's corporations and institutions to set up "affirmative action" programs. These programs are designed to increase the percentage of minority workers in a corporation or institution until that percentage is roughly equal to the percentage of minority persons in the population. For example, a court ordered the fire department in Los Angeles County to hire one black and one Mexican-American for every three whites hired, until the percentage of minorities in the department reached 40 percent—the same percentage of minorities in the county's general population.

Sometimes the effort to prevent discrimination against blacks and other minorities results in a different kind of discrimination, known as "reverse discrimination." This means that in trying to ensure a proper racial balance—say of students in a medical school or workers in an auto factory—whites are denied opportunities just because they are white. This sometimes happens even when the white person is better qualified than the black or Hispanic applicant.

The problem of reverse discrimination is a difficult one, and is only now beginning to be tested in the courts. A final solution to this problem may be a long way off.

As for those "lost" Americans—the American Indians—their cry for human rights has gone the longest unheeded. The Indians were the first real Americans, arriving on the continent of North America some 20,000 to 35,000 years ago —long before whites came looking for land. The Indians moved freely, killed buffalo for food, clothing, and shelter, and were a proud people who taught their children to be honorable and brave.

In 1787, as white people began to spread out and settle the wilderness, the United States government promised the Indians in a declaration called the Northwest Ordinance that "their lands and property shall never be taken from them without their consent." But then, forty-three years later, in 1830, the government departed from that policy, using the Indian Removal Act to force the Indians from their land. The Indians were pushed farther and farther west, onto smaller and smaller areas.

After the discovery of gold in California in 1848, the situation grew even worse. The whites were developing overland routes to the Pacific and destroying the buffalo. In the 1850s and 1860s the Indians fought the whites in a series of wars. But after the Battle of Wounded Knee in 1890, the Indians were forced to give up their struggle, and they were moved onto reservations. Suffering from poor health, lacking in education, and unable to adjust to the white people's ways, they passed through decade after decade of humiliation.

In the 1950s and 1960s, when black Americans began to press for civil rights, the Indians, too, became more vocal in their quest for a better share of human rights. The Department of the Interior began ending federal control over the Indians' reservations, and various efforts were made to give the Indians equal opportunities in housing and employment.

And now?

The Indians are still struggling for full human rights. Their main problem: unemployment, with discrimination against them because they are so "different." As one Indian complained, "Some people still refer to us as 'bucks' and 'squaws.' It's not as bad as the signs that used to say 'No

Reservation life remains bleak and unhealthy for many native American Indians.

*Migrant children working in
a field in North Carolina.*

dogs or Indians Allowed', but it's still a part of our unemployment problem—that and a lack of education and work skills."

Migrant workers are another special group in the United States who often have their human rights trampled upon. Migrant workers are individuals who migrate, or move, from one place to another in order to find work. They may roam, for example, from state to state in the United States to follow the picking seasons for various fruits. Many of the migrants are of Mexican origin, and because of this and the fact that they are always on the move, employers often take advantage of them, paying them little and allowing them to work under the poorest conditions. "Anyone who seems foreign looking, who speaks with an accent and has dark skin, will be discriminated against by employers," said the spokesman for one Mexican-American group that is trying to improve the pay and working conditions for these workers. The U.S. Equal Employment Opportunity Commission also is trying to right some of the wrongs committed against migrant workers.

What can be done about racial discrimination in general?

The General Assembly of the United Nations has condemned it as a violation of human rights and as an obstacle to friendly relations between nations. It has formed a Committee on the Elimination of Racial Discrimination. But, as in the case of human rights generally, the United Nations cannot force governments and peoples to comply with its wishes. No committee, no resolution, and no government even can stamp out the evils of racial discrimination. Only people can do this. Only people themselves can change the way they view one another.

RELIGIOUS FREEDOM

In the sixteenth century, a scholar and theologian named Erasmus uttered what was probably one of the wisest comments ever to be made about religion. "Every definition is a misfortune," he observed. "Enquire if you will, but do not define."

There is still no generally accepted definition of religion. Yet in order to talk about religious freedom, a definition we must have. Therefore, let us say that religion is an identification with, or faith in, something beyond ourselves. Whether we observe a belief in one God or many gods, for instance, it can be said that we are adhering to a religion.

What if *you* had been born into a different faith? What if, instead of believing as a Protestant, a Catholic, or a Jew, you were raised as a Muslim, a Shintoist, or a Hindu?

Wouldn't you still consider yourself rich in religious life and spirit?

To answer yes is to indicate that you believe in the right of people to worship as they wish. The United Nations' Universal Declaration of Human Rights proclaims this principle —the right of everyone, everywhere, to have freedom of religion.

"This right," the Declaration asserts, "shall include freedom [for every person] to have or to adopt a religion or belief of his choice, and freedom, either individually or in community with others and in public or private, to manifest his religion or belief in worship, observance, practice, and teaching."

The United Nations later went even further; it published a document called an International Convention on the Elimination of All Forms of Intolerance and of Discrimination Based on Religion or Belief. This was to proclaim to all nations that freedom of thought and conscience was considered by the U.N. to be a primary human right.

And yet, according to the organization called Amnesty International, which received the Nobel peace prize in 1977, the right to observe one's religious beliefs is denied today by dozens of governments around the world. Even in countries where freedom of religious worship is "guaranteed" by the constitutions of those countries, that freedom is not always granted.

In Communist countries in particular there can be found a flagrant disregard for religious traditions. In the Soviet Union, for example, organized religious instruction is forbidden. There, people punished for professing their beliefs (political as well as religious) are called "prisoners of conscience."

The government does not respond to outside criticism, because communism as a doctrine discourages belief in a Creator of the universe.

All religions in the Soviet Union suffer from the antireligious policies of the Communist party. When, for instance, an Orthodox priest, Father Gleb Yakunin (his real name), criticized the government in his sermons for its antireligious attitudes, he was removed from his parish in Moscow. Yet some religious groups, particularly the Buddhists, Baptists, and Jews, are treated far more harshly than this. Publication of the Holy Scriptures, for example, is forbidden. There are between 2.5 and 3 million Jews in Russia today; yet only a token number of synagogues, no more than a few dozen, are permitted. Jews are allowed no newspapers or magazines of special Jewish interest, no social clubs or official organizations of their own, and they may not hold any public meetings. Anyone caught teaching the Hebrew language faces the threat of prosecution, and all persons who attend Jewish religious services are registered by the Soviet authorities. Jews who apply to emigrate—leave the country—face instant loss of their jobs. They are permitted to emigrate, but at a rate of only 60,000 a year. This means that it could take thirty-five years for all the Jews to leave.

Anti-Semitism—hostility toward or discrimination against Jews—is a worldwide human rights problem, but nowhere today is it as severe as in the Soviet Union.

Why this inhumane treatment of Jews? An American observer offered this explanation: "To Soviet officials, Jews are associated with liberal ideas. They are [also] the one minority group in the country with international links. As such, they are always [open to charges] of spying and trying to undermine the Soviet state."

At the other extreme is the United States, where the highest degree of religious freedom is allowed. In America, all forms of religious expression are found. Part of the reason there is so much freedom of religion in the United States is that its Constitution calls for separation of church and state. That is, the government may not interfere with religious liberty. The First Amendment to the Constitution says, in part, "Congress shall make no law respecting an establishment of religion, or prohibiting the free exercise thereof. . . ." The effect of this Amendment is to make the government neutral in almost all religious matters.

Throughout history many wars have been waged over religion, especially in countries whose governments showed a preference for one religion over another. In 1562, for example, the Protestant Huguenots of France were so cruelly treated that they took up arms to achieve freedom of worship. Between 1562 and 1598, no fewer than eight separate wars were waged between Huguenots and Catholics. Not until 1787 was full religious toleration for Protestants attained in France. From 1618 to 1648 the Catholics and Protestants of Germany waged the Thirty Years' War. It is estimated that as many as seven million people—three-quarters of the German-speaking population—died in the savage fighting of this agonizing struggle.

With their long tradition of religious freedom, American church groups are accustomed to showing concern over persecutions taking place in the world today. For instance, the Human Rights Office of the National Council of Churches of Christ, which represents thirty-one Protestant denominations and has forty million Protestant and Orthodox members, has investigated human rights threats and violations throughout the world. The Human Rights Office has looked into cases in the Philippines, South Korea, Thailand, Paraguay, Chile, Bolivia, Cuba, El Salvador, Argentina, South Africa, and Iran.

What about religious toleration for *non*believers? True religious freedom implies a guarantee concerning even the freedom *not* to believe in God.

The greatest tolerance people can have, it seems, is to understand that the real meaning of religious freedom involves simply the freedom to follow one's conscience. As one professor of religion recently put it, that freedom "ought to be extended to individuals and groups without exception, whether their beliefs and practices arise from affiliation with a Christian church, a Buddhist temple, the Society for Ethical Culture, the American Philosophical Association, or the Flat Earth Society."

WOMEN'S RIGHTS

In Saudi Arabia, women who appear in public without their traditional long dress may be punished by having their legs sprayed with black paint. In many Hindu households in India, the birth of a son is celebrated with joy; the birth of a daughter is greeted with sorrow. In the Philippines and Uruguay, a woman cannot sign a contract or bring a lawsuit without permission from her husband. In Kuwait, Saudi Arabia, and Yemen, women still do not have the right to vote.

About half of the world's population is female. But in nearly every nation of the world there still can be found discrimination against women—simply because they are women.

"God created women to take care of men and children."

"A woman's place is in the home."

"A woman is nobody. A wife is everything."

So go the beliefs of those who advance the theory of male superiority.

"The whole education of women ought to be relative to men. To please them, to be useful to them, to make themselves loved and honored by them, to educate them when young, to care for them when grown, to counsel them, to make life sweet and agreeable to them—these are the duties of women at all times, and what should be taught them from their infancy." These sentiments were expressed in 1762 by Jean Jacques Rousseau, a Frenchman whose writings helped to inspire the French Revolution.

This kind of thinking may be as old as civilization itself. Certainly, it has been with us a long time. In colonial America, for example, a man could buy a wife for tobacco—about 120 pounds (54 kg) worth of it. Women could not vote, hold public office, or sign contracts. It was not until the emergence of the Industrial Revolution in the nineteenth century—when job opportunities opened in industry—that American and European women began to break away from the home.

Women's suffrage—the right of women to vote—became a political issue in America around the turn of the century. Some five thousand American women marched down Pennsylvania Avenue in Washington, D.C., one day in 1913, demanding the right to vote. As they paraded, a group of angry men spat on them and threw lighted cigars and cigarettes at them. It took seven more years for the Nineteenth Amendment to the U.S. Constitution to pass. That Amendment stated: "The right of citizens of the United States to vote shall not be denied or abridged on account of sex." British women won the same right eight years later. But not until 1944 did French women win it.

Susan B. Anthony, perhaps the best-known American

leader of that struggle, died in 1906. That was fourteen years before the Nineteenth Amendment was passed. Today, Anthony is being recognized for her role in American history by having her likeness appear on the new one dollar coin. She is the first American woman to appear on any U.S. currency.

Focusing worldwide attention on the problem of discrimination against women, the United Nations in 1967 adopted a Declaration on the Elimination of Discrimination Against Women. This document urged that all U.N. members make certain that in employment there should be equal pay for both men and women. Similarly, the Declaration stressed that all women should have the right to vote, should be eligible for election, and should have the right to take part in public functions on equal terms with men.

In the United States, in 1966, Betty Friedan and others founded the National Organization for Women (NOW). This activist group hoped to end sex discrimination by bringing pressure to bear on government, industry, and business. Other groups such as Women's Equity Action League and Women United have also formed to help women achieve equal rights. These groups have only partly succeeded.

To help achieve their goals, NOW and other women's rights groups have been urging the passage of a new Amendment to the Constitution. The so-called Equal Rights Amendment (ERA), it is hoped, would eliminate sex as a factor in determining legal rights. It would say, in part: "Equality of rights under the law shall not be denied on account of sex." For the Amendment to be ratified—written into law—it must be formally approved by thirty-eight states. At the time of this writing, thirty-five had already done so. ERA supporters have until 1986 to get three more states behind it.

There are some groups that oppose the passage of ERA.

Many people—including many women—fear that ERA will encourage the breakdown of traditional American family life. Others link the abortion issue—the right of women to end unwanted pregnancies—to ERA. Still others fear that ERA will result in women being drafted into the armed forces or that men will no longer be forced to pay child support. It is difficult to say just how many of these fears, and others concerning ERA, are justified.

Even before ERA, however, women in America were working to improve their position. For many years, for example, women were kept out of many male-dominated professions. They were denied the schooling that would have given them proper training for the jobs. Then, in 1972, Congress ruled that colleges and universities that did not give equal opportunities to men and women would be in danger of losing federal support. As a result, thousands of women are today attending the nation's law, business, medical, and engineering schools, and it is expected that by 1985 the number of women professional and technical workers in the United States will have increased by 18 percent.

The outlook is not all encouraging, however. Black women in America—who have had to fight two kinds of prejudice—are finding it especially tough to win equal rights for themselves in the area of job opportunity.

What about the situation outside the United States? Well, in many parts of the world there is still a lot of the old thinking

Betty Friedan, a founder of NOW and an active feminist.

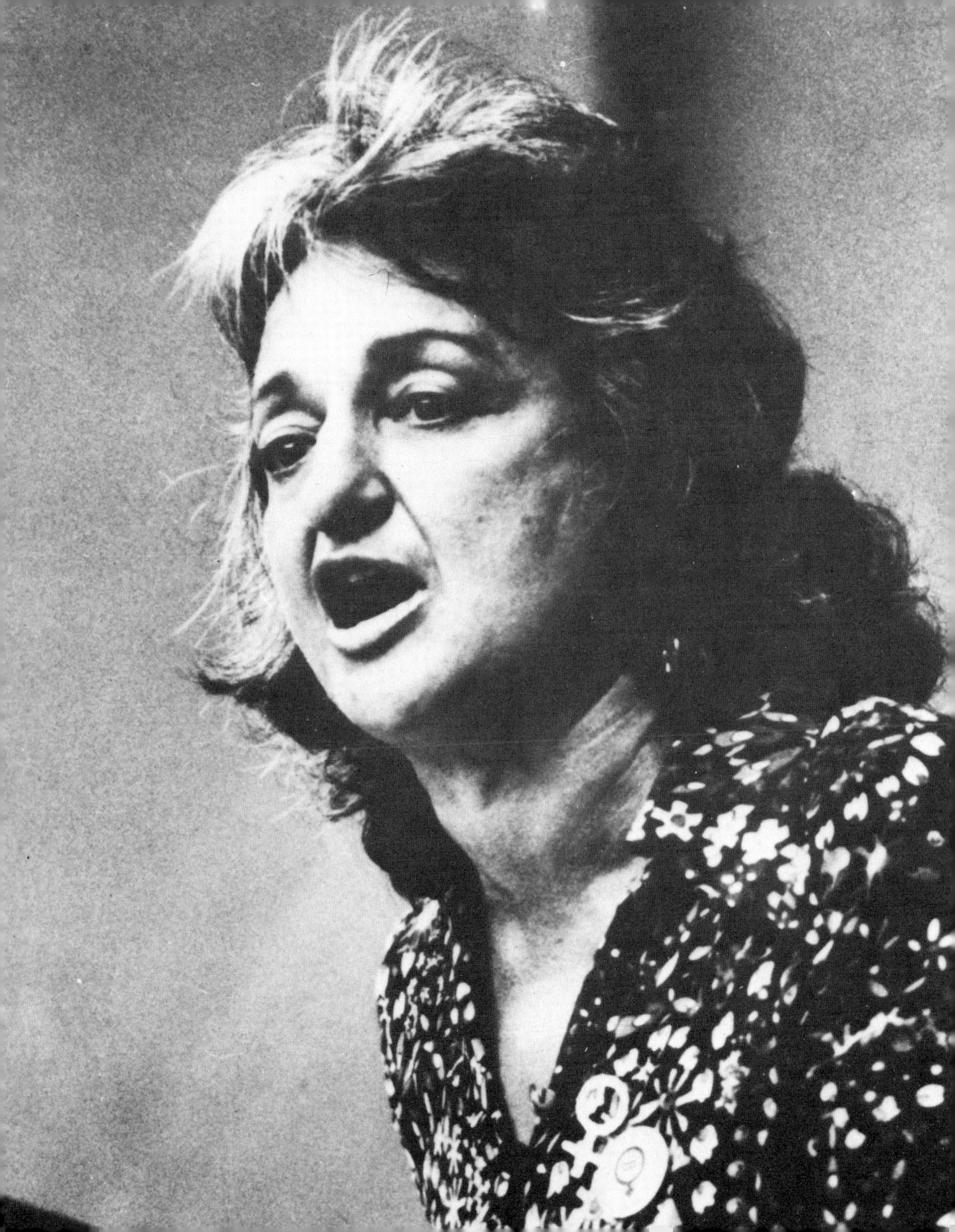

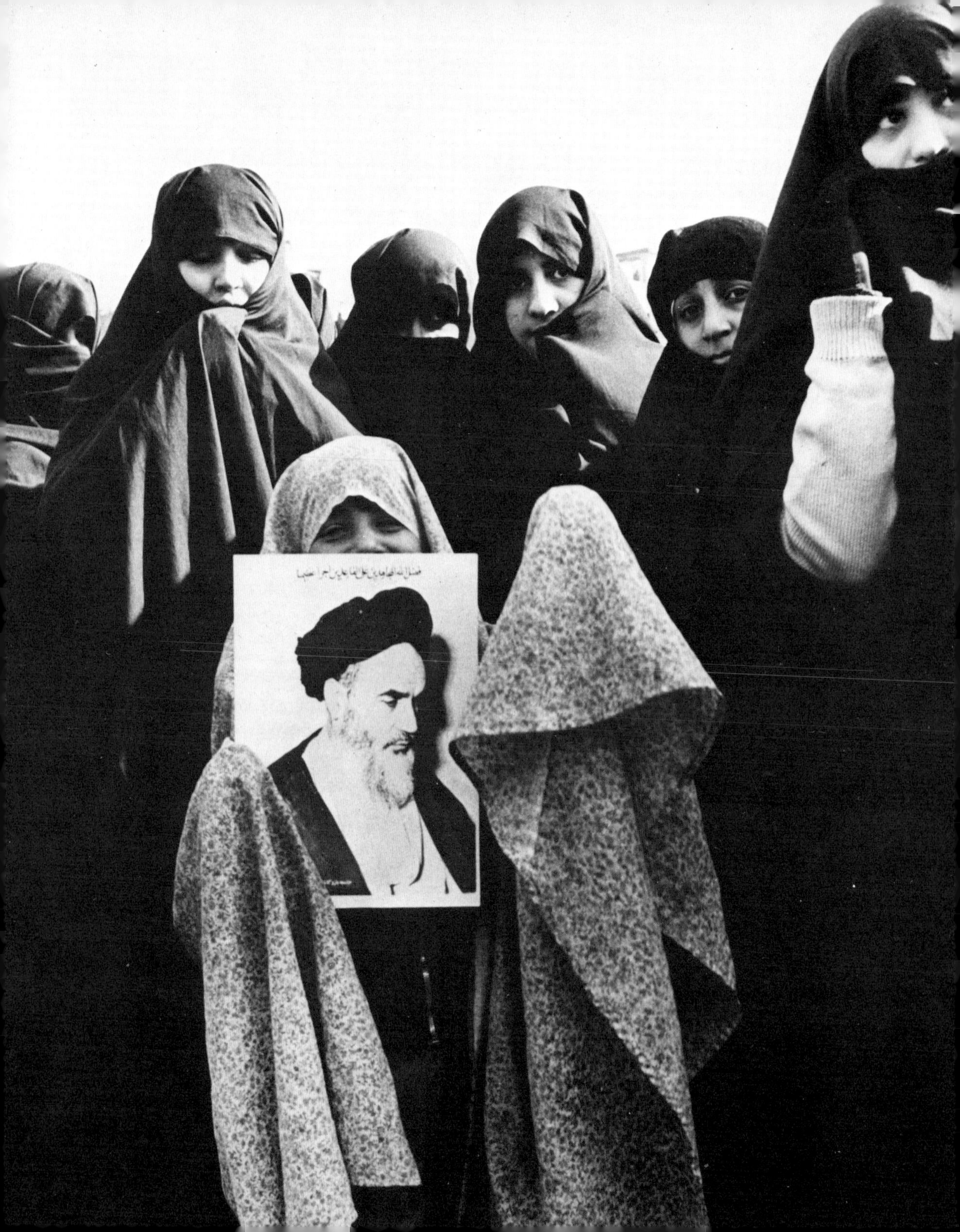

—thinking that for centuries has kept women oppressed. But the winds of change are sweeping a lot of this away.

Among the world's 300 million Muslim women, for example, the traditional veil—the *chuddar*—has long symbolized the lack of freedom for women in male-dominated Muslim societies. Today, less than 20 percent of Muslim women wear the veil, and it does seem like a relic of the past.

However, there are still many Muslims who adhere to the beliefs of the past. When the Shah of Iran, Mohammed Riza Pahlavi, was overthrown and the religious leader, the Ayatollah Ruhollah Khomeini was installed in his place, many women who had discarded the veil put it back on to show their commitment to tradition. At the same time, other women, mostly among the better educated, put on the chuddar to *protest* the threat to their existing freedoms. These women had entered the universities and offices of Iran and feared that a return to strict tradition would rob them of their newfound liberties.

In India, with the coming of independence from Britain in 1947, there came also a cry for the emergence of women from centuries of exploitation. Women were encouraged by the leader of the country's independence movement, Mahatma Gandhi, who said: "To call women the weaker sex is a libel; it is man's injustice to woman. If by strength is meant moral power, then woman is immeasurably man's superior. Has she not got greater intuition, is she not more self-sacri-

Women wearing the traditional dress of Iran march in support of the Ayatollah Khomeini.

ficing, has she not got greater powers of endurance, has she not got greater courage? Without her, man could not be."

Indeed, in modern India, women have prospered in many areas. In the sphere of politics alone, for example, there have already been a number of women who were governors, chief ministers, and legislators. There has even been a woman Prime Minister, Indira Ghandi.

Old prejudices take a long time to die, however. While it is true that India's constitution gives women equal rights with men, the centuries-old principle that a woman's main role is as daughter, sister, wife, and mother still prevails. Some even cling to the ancient Hindu belief that unless a woman bears children who grow up and pray for her reincarnation (rebirth of the soul in another body), her soul will remain damned forever.

"Go, you are divorced!" By just shouting this command at his wife, an Egyptian man used to be able to break the bonds of marriage.

Now this is no longer possible, for in 1979 Egypt's President, Anwar Sadat, signed into law a new civil status decree which makes it necessary for a *Maazoun,* a Muslim priest concerned with marriage and divorce, to be consulted before any divorce can take place.

The decree allows men to continue to take as many as four wives. But now, at least, the man must secure the permission of his first wife.

In China, there used to be an old saying: "A wife is like a horse; you can order her about or beat her as you please." Today, however, there is a real effort to give Chinese women equality with men. China's Youth League newspaper has recently been campaigning against marriage contracts—in which the bride is "bought" with gifts of money and rice from the bridegroom's parents.

In the Arab League countries there is now an Arab Commission on Women. In Italy there is a National Commission on Women's Employment Problems. In France there is a junior Cabinet post of Secretary of State for the Status of Women, and the French Minister of Health, Simone Veil, is considered by some to be a prime candidate in the years ahead for the position of France's first woman Prime Minister. Great Britain, in 1979, elected its first woman Prime Minister, Margaret Thatcher. Portugal, too, has its first woman Prime Minister, Maria De Lurdes Pintassilgi. And in numerous other countries, including Indonesia, Colombia, India, Canada, and Sweden, there are now advisory groups and councils set up to advance the cause of women.

We can now say definitely that human rights as they apply to women are being fought for all around the world, though it may be some time before they are completely won.

CHILDREN'S RIGHTS AND RIGHTS OF THE HANDICAPPED

In the village of Chagoua, in the African country of Chad, a small boy sits, waiting for medical attention. He has leprosy, contracted from an adult. In Africa, Asia, and South America, an estimated fifteen million people suffer from this disease, and hundreds of millions of children run the risk of infection. In the next five years at least half a million children will show symptoms of leprosy.

Across the world, in a rural tar-paper shack in the state of Maine, an American girl sits, waiting for her mother to come home. Her shack has no plumbing. She has never slept in a bed. She has never seen a doctor. And she is cold, for there is no heat. She could freeze to death.

Throughout the world there are hungry and cold children, millions of boys and girls in need of medical attention. In the Philippines, some three million children are suffering from malnutrition; only 20 percent of Filipino preschoolers are in good health. In other countries, little is being done to prevent disease. Disabled in childhood, many children remain disabled all of their lives. Five of the major childhood diseases—diphtheria, whooping cough, tetanus, measles, and polio—can all be prevented, but in the developing countries of the world less than 10 percent of the eighty million children born each year are being immunized against them.

Not all of the ills affecting children are health-related. There are children of school age who cannot read or write, who are in foster homes or institutions without parents, who are abused by their parents, or who are forced to work. According to the International Labor Organization, some fifty-two million children worldwide under the age of fifteen are working.

The year 1979 was officially designated as the International Year of the Child, the name given it by a resolution of the General Assembly of the United Nations. The purpose: to place children, especially young children, in the spotlight of world attention.

The year was chosen because it was the twentieth anniversary of the adoption of the General Assembly's Declaration of the Rights of the Child, a historic document which affirms the rights of the child:

To enjoy special protection; to be given opportunities to develop in a healthy and normal manner and in conditions of freedom; to have a name and a nationality from birth; to enjoy adequate nutrition, housing, recreation, and medical services; to receive education and care if handicapped; to grow up wherever possible in the care of parents; to receive education; to be protected against neglect and cruelty; to be protected from any form of discrimination; and to be brought up in a spirit of understanding, tolerance, friendship among peoples, peace, and universal brotherhood.

In summary, the Declaration states that the human race "owes to the Child the best it has to give."

In Rome, the Vatican City newspaper *L'Osservatore Romano* agreed. It said: "The problem of the well-being of children is one of the largest problems mankind is called upon to resolve. The responsibility for solving these problems does not lie with the family alone, or even with national or international organizations. Because children are our future, they are the responsibility of the whole human race."

Most admit that children's rights must be safeguarded. The fact is, however, that children have few ways of protecting their own rights. If, say, an adult threatens another adult with a large stick, he or she would be arrested for assault—an unlawful attempt to harm another person. But if the threat is made against a child, it is too often accepted as all right.

In every state in the United States, child abuse—which generally refers to child beating or the inflicting of physical harm—is a crime. But only infrequently are abusive parents brought before the law. The reason for this is that the states cannot, or will not, intrude on the private life of the family.

Child abuse is a long-standing practice. For hundreds of years, all over the world, children were regarded as private

A lonely Peruvian child waits for her mother to finish work in the corn field.

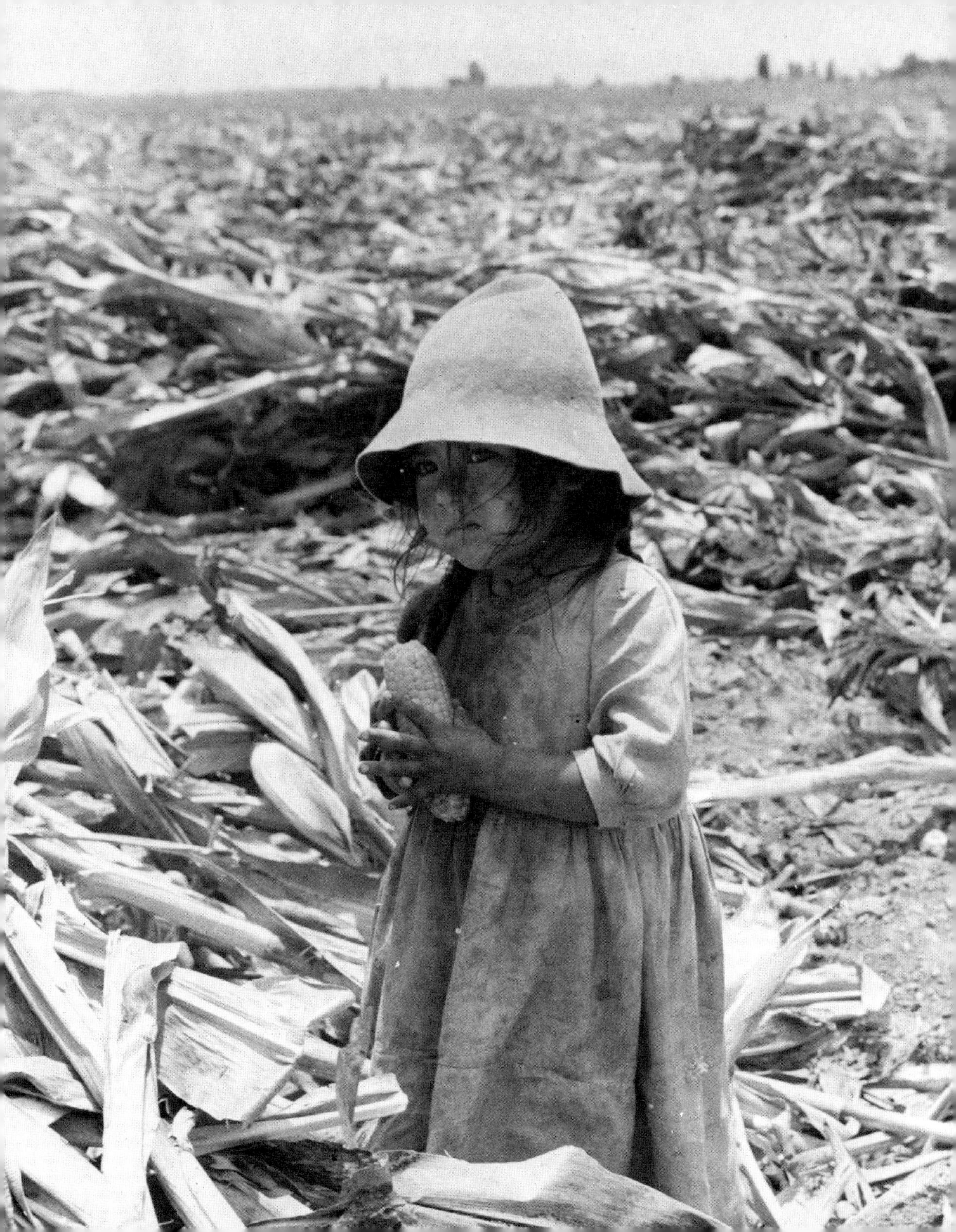

Left: a Venezuelan child laborer.
Right: being denied an education is
a serious human rights violation.
But often it is the lack of
teachers and teaching equipment that
makes this violation so widespread.
Here, a Sudanese schoolboy
writes his lesson in the sand.

property. In some countries, children, especially girls, used to be thrown into rivers or tossed into gutters to be left to die. In some parts of the world it was common to use children in begging, and since a child who was handicapped would show greater profits, many parents purposely mutilated their own children. Not until the nineteenth century, in both Europe and America, did the common practice of whipping children die out. But still common is the practice of beating children to force discipline on them.

With the worldwide emergence of the fight for women's rights in the late nineteenth and early twentieth centuries, the status of the child gradually improved. Child labor laws and compulsory education served to advance the welfare of children everywhere.

Yet child abuse can still be found even in the most advanced countries. In Britain, for instance, the National Society for the Prevention of Cruelty to Children recently released an annual report that the organization's spokesman described as "a record of twelve months' neglect and deterioration on a scale that rips away the tissue veneer of our so-called civilized society. Yet the full horror of this national scandal may never be known, for we can speak only of the incidents that were brought to our notice."

Among these incidents: a three-year-old girl was plunged into a bath of scalding water; a four-month-old baby was beaten until it suffered four fractured ribs and broken arms; a one-and-a-half-year-old boy was beaten by his father with a wire whip; a boy of eight was burned all over his body with cigarettes.

The spokesman added, "Other children had been starved and neglected or were found living in circumstances so squalid as to defy adequate description."

To combat such abuse in the United States, many Americans are fighting for new laws they think will better protect the child. Groups that have shown special concern in this area include the National Alliance for the Prevention and Treatment of Child Abuse and Maltreatment, the Junior League, the League of Women Voters, the Young Men's Christian Association, the Girl Scouts of America, various child abuse task forces, and local departments of social services as well as many individual doctors, social workers, and lawyers.

Divorce is often a factor in child abuse, with children suffering from the frustrations of their parents. In the United States there are well over 600,000 divorces each year involving children, and in an estimated 100,000 of these cases young people become the victims of "child-snatching"—the practice some divorced parents have of stealing and hiding their children from each other. Snatching or abducting a child against his or her will interferes with the child's personal liberty and can cause serious mental harm.

Many groups concerned with this problem, such as United Parents of Absconded Children, Parents of Kidnapped Children, and Men's Equality Now, believe the Federal Kidnapping Act passed in 1971 should include child-snatching as a crime. It does not. Thus, the Federal Bureau of Investigation cannot be turned to for help. However, about half of the fifty states have now passed into law the Uniform Child Custody Jurisdiction Act. Essentially, this law makes custody rights apply even outside the state in which they were drawn up.

Many children—and adults—face a threat to their human rights because they are handicapped. There are an estimated 35 million handicapped adult Americans and an additional 5.5 million handicapped children of school age. Like handicapped adults, handicapped children suffer from a variety of impairments, including blindness, deafness, paralysis, mental retardation, and so on. Two million children have orthopedic —bone—deformities.

The handicapped, both adult and child, need special equipment and services to cope with their disabilities. In the 1970s, the handicapped have become quite assertive in claiming their right—their human right—to get the help they need.

Slowly, the pleas of the handicapped are being heard. There are now automatic door openers for the home, telephones that can be activated by the sound of a voice and do not have to be lifted by hand, and eating utensils with bicycle-grip handles for those whose fingers cannot hold the customary spoons, knives, or forks.

But the handicapped, and particularly young people who are handicapped, need much more. By federal law, all handicapped children are entitled to a "free appropriate public education." But there are too few trained teachers available to teach them, too few texts in Braille—the system of writing for the blind that uses characters made up of raised dots—too few ramps to help the disabled get around. The problem in America, as elsewhere in the world, is at least partly money. Vast sums are needed for new equipment—buses with special lifts for the wheelchair-bound, for example, and Braille books and Braille typewriters.

By focusing attention on children, the International Year of the Child has helped to create an awareness of this problem and others. It has also been able to induce nations worldwide to reexamine and improve their services for children, handicapped or otherwise.

Egypt, India, and Jordan are reviewing their own services

for children through national surveys, discussion groups, and community workshops. The Federal Republic of Germany, New Zealand, Sudan, and Sweden have established groups to examine such issues as violence and accidents in the home. In the United States, some lawyers have formed the National Association of Counsel for Children to make sure that children are treated fairly by the law.

In all, more than one hundred countries have established national commissions to study children's rights.

In Berkeley, California, the board of directors of an organization called EVAN-G (End Violence Against the Next Generation) enthusiastically supports the concept of the International Year. To the Declaration of the Rights of the Child, the group has proposed the addition of one more right —"the right to be assured of the integrity of their own bodies from intrusions by whips, paddles, straps, and other instruments mistakenly believed to be educational."

The rights extolled in the Declaration are not yet available to all children, not even to most children. Almost half of the world's young people still grow up without an education. Four out of every ten adults still cannot read or write. Progress is being made, however. Governments all the world over are at least agreeing that special assistance to children—and to the handicapped—is not a luxury to be given but a duty owed.

WHAT CAN THE UNITED NATIONS DO?

We have already seen that the United Nations is very much involved in the struggle for human rights. In San Francisco on December 10, 1945, when the founders of the United Nations met to draw up a charter, they established immediately the link between respect for human rights and human survival:

WE THE PEOPLES OF
THE UNITED NATIONS DETERMINED
to save succeeding generations from the scourge of war, which twice in our lifetime has brought untold sorrow to mankind, and to reaffirm faith in fundamental human rights, in the dignity and worth of the human person, in the equal rights of men and women and of nations large and small . . .

These words are from the preamble—the preface—to the United Nations' Charter. Only out of a basic respect for human rights, the delegates felt, could future generations be spared the scourge of war.

Three years later, without one dissenting vote, the General Assembly of the United Nations adopted the Universal Declaration of Human Rights. This historic document proclaims: "All human beings are born free and equal in dignity and rights. They are endowed with reason and conscience and should act toward one another in a spirit of brotherhood."

Furthermore, said the Declaration, "Everyone has the right to life, liberty, and security of person . . . no one shall be held in slavery . . . no one shall be subjected to torture or to cruel, unhuman, or degrading treatment or punishment . . . all are equal before the law and are entitled without any discrimination to equal protection of the law . . . everyone charged with a penal offense has the right to be presumed innocent until proven guilty . . . everyone has the right to freedom of movement and residence within the borders of each state . . . everyone has the right to leave any country, including his own, and to return to his country . . . everyone has the right to own property . . . everyone has the right to freedom of thought, conscience, and religion . . . everyone has the right to take part in the government of his country."

Many countries have agreed to follow the principles set forth in the Declaration, and in the constitutions of some countries the Declaration's wording is reflected. But the Declaration is not a binding set of rules. That is, each country, on its own, has the final say in human rights matters. No international body, not even the United Nations, can override the authority of the government of a sovereign nation. As the U.N. itself notes, countries "consider that matters like human

THE UNIVERSAL DECLARATION of Human Rights

rights are best decided in accordance with their own procedures and laws and customs."

But if this is so, if the U.N. cannot send an army in to enforce the granting of human rights, what good is the Universal Declaration of Human Rights?

The answer is simple: the U.N. has one great power at its command—the power of exposing to world public opinion the wrongdoing of any nation. The problem of protecting and promoting human rights is the main concern of the U.N. Each year, for at least a month, the U.N. Commission on Human Rights meets to make recommendations on ways of promoting human rights. At that time it attempts to settle disagreements on human rights between nations; but that first great power—to make human rights violations public—is the real weapon with which the United Nations can spark concern over human rights violations.

For example, slavery and practices similar to slavery are still to be found in some parts of the world. The matter is now actively before the U.N., which is trying to end all forms of slavery and practices similar to slavery—such as the purchase of brides and the exploitation of child labor—by making such practices known and subject to public censure.

On other worldwide issues, such as genocide, the U.N. has been effective in attracting world attention to the situation. Genocide means the intent to destroy a national, racial, or religious group and is a crime under international law, whether committed in time of peace or of war. During World War II, for example, the Nazi government of Germany systematically slaughtered millions of innocent people simply because they were Jews. Three years after the war, the United Nations General Assembly adopted and published a document called the Convention on the Prevention and Punishment of the Crime of Genocide, designed to make the governments of the world aware of the monstrous nature of this crime.

Each year, thousands of people turn to the United Nations, complaining of abuses and pleading for help. Most of the pleas come by mail, and from their tone it is evident that the writers feel they may be risking their freedom if the letters should fall into the hands of their own governments.

For example, writers have protested against apartheid in Africa, they have complained about government censorship of the press in Poland, and they have cited restrictions on the rights of people to travel into and out of Hungary. To protect individuals, the United Nations routes all of the letters to a special group that is part of the Subcommission on Human Rights. In a closed session each summer the group goes through all of the complaints and reports to the Subcommission. The group cannot deal with every one, but if a pattern of violations appears—many imprisonments without trials in a certain country, for instance—the incidents are brought before the Subcommission for further study. Then they may become an issue for debate, and any countries cited for human rights violations are named publicly.

Further, the gates of the international organization itself are an inviting target for many protesters. Thus, at the United Nation's world headquarters in New York City on December 10, 1978—on the thirtieth anniversary celebration of Human Rights Day, marking the adoption of the Universal Declaration of Human Rights—hundreds of black demonstrators gathered to protest human rights abuses in the United States. In America today, they charged, blacks are still denied many of the same basic freedoms enjoyed by whites.

Similarly, protesters denouncing "the destruction of democratic institutions," such as the free press in Chile and the Soviet Union, have chosen the U.N. building as a place to make their voices heard. From supporters of Soviet Jewry, the cry, "Let our people go!" also has been given widespread publicity because it is often heard outside U.N. headquarters.

But what can we as individuals do?

First, we must understand what our human rights are. Then, if they are violated, we will recognize the act as a violation. We can also promote human rights—for others as well as for ourselves. One way to do this is to discuss the subject with our family and friends. We can ask teachers about human rights and read articles on the subject in newspapers and magazines. Most important, of course, we can—and must—respect the human rights of others.

INDEX

Abernathy, Ralph, 23
Adams, John Quincy, 13
"Affirmative action" programs, 27
American Indians, discrimination against 27–29
Amin, Idi, 9
Amnesty International, 33
Anthony, Susan B., 38–39
Anti-semitism in Soviet Union, 34
Apartheid, 20, 22–23
    denounced by other nations, 22
    economic value of, 23
    protest against, at U.N., 59
    and sports, 22
Association of American Publishers, 17

Braille, 53

Brecht, Bertolt, 17–18

Carter, Jimmy, 6, 7, 12
Child abuse, 48–53
    divorce as factor in, 52
    long history of, 48–51
    organizations for prevention of, 52
Child labor, 30, 47, 50
"Child snatching," 52
    organizations for prevention of, 53, 54
Children as private property, 48–51
Children's health, problems of, 46–47
Children's rights,
    as defined by the U.N., 47–48
    progress in, 54
    under the law, 54

Chuddar, 42, 43
Civil Rights Act of 1964, 25–26
Civil rights movement, 23
    loss of unity in, 26
    organization prominent in, 25
Committee on the Elimination of Racial Discrimination, 31

Declaration on the Elimination of Discrimination Against Women, 39
Declaration of the Rights of the Child, 47–48, 54

Economic barriers to human rights, 22
Equal Rights Amendment, (ERA), 39
    opposition to, 40
Erasmus, 32

Federal Kidnapping Act, 52
First Amendment, 16
    and separation of church and state, 35
Foreign policy and human rights, 6–7
Freedom House, 2
Friedan, Betty, 39, 41
Fulbright, James William, 12–13

Genocide, 58–59
Ghandi, Mahatma, 43
Ginzburg, Alexander, 17
Gulag Archipelago, The, Solzhenitsyn, 17

Handicapped, rights of, 52–53
    education, 53
    services and equipment, 53
Human Rights Office of the National Council of Churches of Christ, 35

International Labor Organization, 47
International Year of the Child, 53, 54
    purpose of, 47
Interpretation of human rights, 11
    debate about, in U.S., 12–13
    by Jimmy Carter, 6–7, 12
    by the United Nations, 3–4

"Job reservation," 21

Kennedy, John F., 25
Khomeini, Ayatolloh Ruhollah, 42, 43
King, Martin Luther, Jr., 23, 24, 26
Knowlton, Winthrop, 17

Leprosy in children, 46

Malnutrition in children, 11, 47
Map of Freedom, 2
Migrant workers, 30, 31

National Association of Counsel for Children, 54
Nineteenth Amendment, 38, 39

Orlov, 17, 18
L'Osservatore Romano, 48

Pahlavi, Mohammed Riza (Shah), 43

P.E.N. International, 14, 15
Pintassilgi, Maria De Lurdes, 45
Political rights, 8–13
    sovereignty and, 10
Protest marches at U. N., 59–60

Racial discrimination in U.S., 23–28, 59
    condemned by U.N., 31
    in jobs, 27
Racial segregation, 20
    in schools in U.S., 26
Religion defined, 32
Religious discrimination
    against Jews, 34
    in Soviet Union, 33–34
Religious freedom
    true meaning of, 36
    in U.S., 35
"Reverse discrimination," 27
Right to travel, 20, 56, 59
Rousseau, Jean Jacques, 38

Sex discrimination
    in professional education, 40
    See also Women's rights
Slavery, 58
Solzhenitsyn, Alexander, 17, 18
South Africa, 20, 21, 22–23
    See also Apartheid
Sovereignty and human rights, 10, 56
Soviet Union
    freedom of expression in, 12, 17
Sports and apartheid, 22

Steinberger, Thomas, 15
Suarez, Eugenio, 15
Subcommission on Human Rights, 59

Thatcher, Margaret, 45
Torture, 8

Uniform Child Custody Jurisdiction Act, 52
United Nations, 3, 31, 33, 39, 47, 54
United Nations Charter, preamble to, 55–56
United Nations and human rights
    handling of protests, 59–60
    history of, 55–56
    and world public opinion, 58
    See also Subcommission on Human Rights
U.S. Equal Employment Opportunity Commission, 26, 31
Universal Declaration of Human Rights, 33, 56, 58, 59

Veil, Simone, 45
Voting rights, 25, 37, 38–39

Women's rights, 40–45
    organizations in support of, 39
    and status of the child, 51
Writers, punishment of, 10–11, 14–15
Wurtman, Judith J., 32

Zimbabwe-Rhodesia, 21, 22

ABOUT THE AUTHOR

Gerald S. Snyder is the author of numerous children's books. His work has been cited for excellence by the National Science Teachers Association, the Children's Book Council, and the National Council for Social Studies. His articles have been published in many magazines, including *Junior Scholastic*. A former newsman for United Press International in New York, Mr. Snyder has lived in Maryland for most of the last twelve years.